Croydon

IN OLD PHOTOGRAPHS

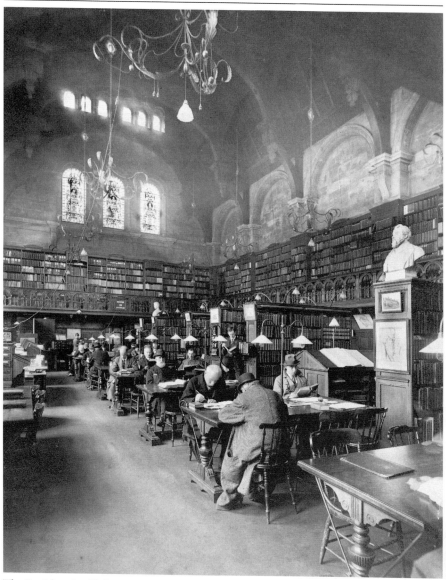

The Braithwaite Hall, 1922. The hall, which housed Croydon's Reference Library until 1993, was named after Revd John Masterman Braithwaite who was vicar of Croydon between 1883 and 1889. His daughter Lilian became a famous actress and was eventually made a Dame.

Opposite: North End, *c*. 1890, showing the police station on the left and Freeman, Hardy and Willis on the right. Just past the police station on the left is Kennards the Drapers, which was opened by William Kennard in 1851 and later became Debenhams.

Croydon

IN OLD PHOTOGRAPHS

STUART BLIGH

FROM THE PHOTOGRAPHIC COLLECTION AT
CROYDON LOCAL STUDIES LIBRARY

Alan Sutton Publishing Limited
Phoenix Mill · Far Thrupp · Stroud
Gloucestershire

First published 1994

FOR NORMAN RICHARD BLIGH

British Library Cataloguing in Publication Data.
A catalogue record for this book is available from
the British Library.

ISBN 0-7509-0739-8

Typeset in 9/10 Sabon.
Typesetting and origination by
Alan Sutton Publishing Limited.
Printed and bound in Great Britain by
WBC, Bridgend, Mid Glam.

Crowds waiting in Union Road to greet King George V and Queen Mary on the
occasion of their visit to Gillett and Johnston's bell foundry in May 1925. The Old Mail
Coach pub is visible in the background on the corner of Union and Whitehorse Roads.

Contents

Croydon Camera Club Excursion to Wickham Court, May 1890. This photograph was taken only shortly after the club was officially formed in March of the same year, possibly during its first official outing. The club was set up in response to growing calls for such a body as photography became more and more popular in the area. The reclining gentleman looks very like Hector MacLean, the founder and first chairman of the club, and a well-known photographer in the area.

Introduction

The London Borough of Croydon has a rich and diverse history. This fact is perhaps not appreciated by many who see the town as a purely modern place, created by the massive development of the 1950s and '60s. In fact, although the very early history of the town is not clear, there was certainly some sort of settlement here before Roman times. However, it is likely that the town became properly established during the Roman occupation as a 'mansio' or staging post on one of the main Roman roads out of London and later became a Saxon settlement based near where the parish church is today. This early start gave Croydon the impetus to become an important market town in Surrey by the seventeenth century when it put in its first (unsuccessful) request for incorporation. Another factor that was important in the development of the town was the Church. The Archbishop of Canterbury probably owned an estate around Croydon from before 800 and ever since the town has had strong connections with the archbishops. It is recorded that a synod was held in Croydon in 809, which indicates that the place was quite important in a religious context. The Old Palace, which still exists today and is on the site of what was probably the original manor house, became the summer residence of the archbishops as it lay conveniently on the route between Lambeth and Canterbury. As such, several royal visitors were entertained there, including, most famously, Elizabeth I.

The town continued to expand throughout the Middle Ages but it was not until the early nineteenth century that it began to evolve as the important commercial and business centre it is today. The catalyst for this was, as in many other places, the arrival of the railway from London in 1839. Croydon's population grew from about 16,000 in 1841 to around 133,000 in 1901, a rise of over 800 per cent! The town was one of the first to adopt the Public Health Act of 1849 and set up a Local Board of Health, which meant that by the end of the 1870s Croydon had one of the most efficient water supply, drainage and sewage systems in the country. This in itself was enough to attract people to Croydon but its still predominantly rural setting also made it a much sought after location for early commuters to London. These new residents were, in the main, wealthy business and professional people, and their presence obviously increased the town's standing still further. Finally, in 1883, Croydon received the Charter of Incorporation allowing it to elect a mayor and a municipal borough council and this was the beginning of the modern borough of Croydon.

Growth continued throughout the first half of the twentieth century but the next, and perhaps most important and influential stage of Croydon's development came after the Second World War. Croydon suffered extensively from bomb damage during the war. In fact it was the most fly-bombed of all the London boroughs, with 141 bombs landing over a ten-week period in 1944. Apart from this a total of 2,621 other bombs were dropped on the town between 1940 and 1944 causing 523 fatalities and a total of 1,200 buildings destroyed. In 1945 Croydon's Reconstruction Committee announced its proposals for the town for the next fifty years. This was to become the basis for the emergence of the 'New Croydon' visualized by the Council in general and its leader Sir James Marshall in particular and was eventually formalized as the Croydon Development Plan of 1951. This plan was approved by central government in 1954 and the next and most controversial stage of the town's development had begun.

The appearance of the town today is basically the result of the planning decisions of the 1950s and '60s with their emphasis on business and commerce, and especially the conscious decision to focus on office development. There are many views regarding the effect this has had on the town, most of them not favourable due to the fact that the rapid development, especially of central Croydon, meant the disappearance of many old and much loved buildings and landmarks.

However, it is precisely this rapid growth of Croydon which makes the collection and preservation of images of the past so necessary and important. The town was fortunate that it had one of the best and most innovative library services in the country in the early part of this century. Librarians such as Louis Stanley Jast, Ernest Savage and W.C. Berwick Sayers, who all worked at Croydon, became nationally famous for their work on and ideas for public libraries. However, it is probably to Jast that we owe most thanks in Croydon for the preservation of the borough's heritage as he was interested in both local history and photography and was one of the founders of the Photographic Survey and Record of Surrey, which began in 1902. As a consequence of Jast's involvement (he was honorary curator) the photographs from the survey were stored at Croydon Library and became a major part of the photographic collection from which most of the photographs in this book have been selected. Jast was in charge of Croydon's libraries between 1898 and 1915, and during his time here he was responsible for a considerable number of innovations, one of which was to set up a local history collection relating to Croydon. This slowly grew to become the Croydon Local History collection with the first specialist local history librarian appointed in 1973. It is a shame that Jast will not be around to see his work culminate in the opening of a brand new purpose-built Local Studies Library at Croydon Central Library in autumn 1994.

In selecting the pictures for this book I have tried to avoid the more photographed and popular areas and buildings in the borough, as these have mostly been included in earlier books. I have also opted to divide the borough up into well-known areas even though in some cases there weren't many photographs relating to the individual area concerned. However, I think this way of organizing the book is justified as it allows readers to identify more closely with areas that are familiar to them. I should add that if anyone looking at these pictures can supply more information or an exact date for them, the staff at Croydon Local Studies Library would be more than happy to hear from them (the same is true for any mistakes that may have occurred!). Please note also that in the West and East Croydon sections of the book there are not only pictures of the areas traditionally known by these names but also of areas that are geographically in east and west Croydon such as Addiscombe and Waddon.

Stuart Bligh
June 1994

SECTION ONE

Norwood and Woodside

E.M. Hughman, captain of Woodside Swimming Club, who later became Sir Montague Hughman, chairman of Henley Cables (see page 10).

Woodside Swimming Club after winning the Surrey County Junior Water Polo Championship in 1906. Founded in 1887 the club was one of the earliest swimming clubs in Croydon.

Norwood Grove, 1804. The house was probably built around this time and its early occupants included William Cavendish Scott (Duke of Portland) and Arthur Anderson, a well-known pioneer of steam shipping. It is still standing today in Norwood Grove Park.

Although not technically in Croydon, this photograph of Anerley Hill in 1900 gives a fine view of the Crystal Palace, which was attracting an average of 870,000 visitors annually at this time, many of them from the Croydon area.

Upper Norwood Recreation Ground with a tower from the Crystal Palace in the background. The recreation ground was opened in May 1890.

Macclesfield Road, South Norwood, *c.* 1916. The first houses appeared in the road in 1905 and this postcard shows Mr Skinner's General Stores on the corner of Macclesfield and Albert Roads.

Frederick Carbery's butcher's shop at No. 29 Westow Street, Upper Norwood, *c.* 1895.

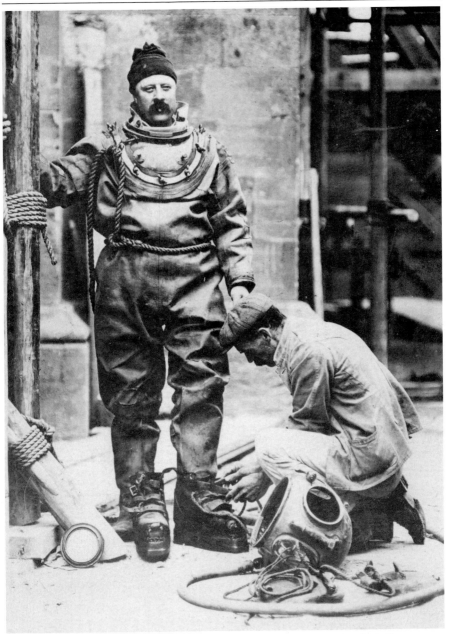

William Walker, the diver who lived in Portland Road, South Norwood. Walker was an ordinary diver who became famous through his restoration work at Winchester Cathedral (1906–11) which involved diving beneath the building to shore up the sinking foundations. He used to cycle to Winchester from South Norwood at the beginning of the week, stay there working during the week and cycle back at the weekend.

The Stanley memorial clock tower in South Norwood High Street, decorated for Christmas 1910. W.F. Stanley was a prominent local citizen and businessman who lived in Lancaster Road, South Norwood. His firm made scientific instruments but Stanley was also an inventor, one of his patents being for a new improved lemon squeezer.

South Norwood High Street, at the junction with Portland Road and South Norwood Hill, decorated for Christmas 1909. The Albion is on the left-hand corner and in the distance the road rises up towards Goat House Bridge.

Westow Hill, Upper Norwood, *c.* 1900. The gap in the shops on the right just before Cooper's Boot Stores was filled by Upper Norwood Wesleyan Methodist Chapel, whose four lanterns can be seen clearly (the chapel itself was set back from the road).

The Beulah Spa Hydro and Residential Hotel, which stood next to the Beulah Spa pub at Beulah Hill, Upper Norwood, until it was demolished shortly before the Second World War.

Westwood, No. 49 Beulah Hill, Upper Norwood, the home of the celebrated Baptist minister Revd C.H. Spurgeon until his death in 1892. Spurgeon was known as the 'Prince of Preachers'.

Station Road in South Norwood, looking down towards Norwood Junction station, c. 1920. The original railway station at Norwood was called Jolly Sailor and opened in 1839; Norwood Junction opened in 1856.

South Norwood's first electric tram in March 1902, probably in South Norwood High Street. This section of Croydon's electric tram-line was one of the last to be opened because of problems caused by the narrowness of the High Street.

Tree lopping from a motor-bus in Crown Lane in 1920. Bus companies held themselves responsible for trimming overhanging branches because of the possible danger to passengers on open-top buses.

A pair-horse bus in South Norwood High Street, *c*. 1898. This particular vehicle belonged to Andrew's Star Omnibus Company.

David Wallace, foreman of the South Norwood Volunteer Fire Brigade, 1886.

Chestnut Farm at Woodside Green, 1905. The farm was run for many years by William Weston and was situated on the corner of Elmers Road and Woodside Green near Woodside Junior School.

South Norwood Recreation Ground, *c.* 1910. This land was acquired by the council in 1889 after complaints that South Norwood was very badly off for recreational space.

Benjamin Wilkinson (by the horse) taking delivery of a new cart from J.A. Clarke, Coach & Cart Manufacturer of Clifton Road, South Norwood, in 1910.

Lt.-Col. G.K.M. Mason addressing a Conservative fête at Woodside Green in 1926. Lt.-Col. Mason was MP for the old parliamentary constituency of Croydon North from 1922 until he retired in 1940.

SECTION TWO

Norbury

Mayor Keatley Moore on a visit to Norbury (see page 27).

Kilmartin Avenue, Norbury, *c.* 1920. The road is one of several in the area named after castles in Scotland (others are Ederline, Dunbar and Melrose) presumably because there was a Scottish ancestor in the family of the developers, Chesterton and Sons.

London Road, Norbury, looking north from Roche Road, *c.* 1905. The road looks much the same as it does today apart from the tram lines and ornate lamp-posts.

Bavant Road, Norbury, *c.* 1920. This road was part of the first London County Council 'out-county' estate built in Norbury just after the turn of the century.

Wounded soldiers from Croydon's military hospitals being entertained at North Surrey Golf Course in Norbury in July 1918. Patients were well looked after by the local community, who organized other events including days out, whist drives and sports days.

Flooding at London Road, Norbury, June 1914. The floods were the result of a storm that 'was so severe that even the most foolhardy would never have dreamt of braving the elements' according to the *Croydon Times*.

The Rex Cinema in London Road, Norbury, which was next to the Norbury Hotel. The cinema opened in 1937 and closed in 1962.

Looking south from where Pollards Hill Recreation Ground is now, *c.* 1914. The houses in the foreground are in Pollards Hill West and are still being built. The completed houses to the right and behind them are in Pollards Hill South.

Workers at the Pollards Hill Brickfields, *c.* 1901. The brickfields may have been located where the recreation ground now is as a clay pit is shown on maps of the area at that time (clay was an essential ingredient for brickmaking).

Green Lane, Norbury, *c.* 1910. Green Lane is one of the oldest roads in Croydon and was part of the original track from London to Croydon through the Great North Wood.

London Road, Norbury, *c.* 1910, showing that much of the western side was still residential at that time.

Norbury Library, Beatrice Avenue, shortly after it opened in May 1931. The first librarian-in-charge was Leonard M. Harrod, who went on to become Chief Librarian of Islington. The membership at Norbury was reported as 'well over 2,000' after the first week.

Croydon's mayor, Councillor Keatley Moore, waiting in his carriage at the borough boundary at Hermitage Bridge, Norbury, for the Lord Mayor of London on the occasion of the opening of the new fire station at Park Lane, Croydon, in November 1906.

W.G. Grace batting against Australia at Norbury Hall in 1888. He was playing fo Gloucestershire at the time but had been enlisted for G.I. Thornton's XI. However, h only managed 10 runs in the first innings and 4 in the second.

Pollards Hill South after a flying bomb attack in July 1944. Altogether three flyin bombs fell on this road, all in July.

SECTION THREE
Thornton Heath

Daytrippers outside the Bricklayer's Arms (see page 33).

Brigstock Road, Thornton Heath, *c.* 1910, with Thornton Heath railway station in the distance. Brigstock Road was named after the Bryckstocke family, who had a mansion in London Road as early as 1571.

The Parade Boot Repairing Depot, No. 2 The Parade, Wiltshire Road, Thornton Heath, *c.* 1924. The depot was run by Mr Spencer, who is second from the left in this photograph.

Gonville Road, Thornton Heath, *c.* 1920. The road was built around 1900 and is perhaps best known for Gonville School, which was opened in October 1930.

Grangewood Mansion standing in what is now Grange Park, June 1910. The mansion was built in 1861 for Charles Hood and eventually bought by Croydon Corporation in 1901. At this time part of the house was being used as a museum.

The Crescent War Hospital, Selhurst, in the premises of Selhurst Boys' Grammar School, The Crescent, September 1917. Six schools in the Croydon area were used as war hospitals and their pupils relocated at other schools or council buildings.

A photograph of staff and patients during Christmas festivities at The Crescent War Hospital (now Selhurst Tertiary Centre) in 1918. Some of the wounded soldiers are dressed for the Christmas panto.

Ecclesbourne House, No. 107 Bensham Manor Road, which was used as a military hospital during the First World War, seen here in 1917 with the staff taking a break in the sun. The street directories of the time list Miss Cornwall as the matron-in-charge.

A charabanc outing to Brighton from the Bricklayer's Arms on the corner of Northwood and Parchmore Roads, c. 1921.

Boston Road Mission Church Army Band, possibly at the opening of the mission in Christchurch Infants' School, Boston Road, in 1922.

Bensham Lane behind Mayday Hospital, Thornton Heath, *c.* 1907. The road was originally a track across Bensham Common fields.

Beulah Road, Thornton Heath, 1917. The road was built around 1865.

Melfort Road at the junction with Quadrant and Brook Roads, Thornton Heath – from a postcard postmarked 1927.

The Co-Op Milk Depot in Farnley Road in 1922, shortly after it opened. The manager was Mr Feist, who is standing at the front, third from the right. Mr Slatter, who looked after the horses, is on the far left.

Selhurst Park Football Ground (home of Crystal Palace Football Club) shortly after it opened in August 1924. Whitehorse Lane is at the top and Holmesdale Road at the bottom. The Holmesdale Road end at this time was simply a bank of grass.

Thornton Heath railway station before it was rebuilt in 1897. The station was opened in December 1862 as part of the Croydon to Balham line.

Queens Road Cemetery in a photograph probably taken around 1875, as Pawsons Road to the left and Princess Road to the right only have a few houses. The cemetery opened for burials in 1861. Queens Road was apparently known as 'death and poverty street' as it housed both the workhouse and the cemetery.

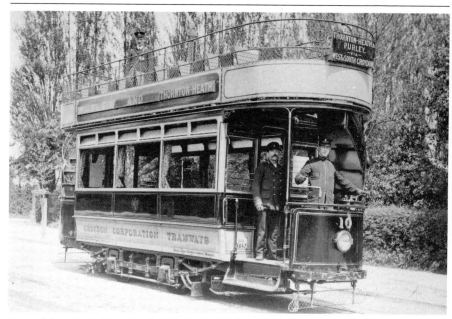

One of the original batch of electric-powered Croydon Corporation tramcars supplied by G.F. Milnes to the Corporation in 1901.

New Year's Eve 1934 at the Thornton Heath Palais de Danse in Thornton Heath High Street. It is a sobering thought looking at all the happy faces that the country would soon be at war again.

May Day celebrations at an unknown school, possibly Beulah Road, *c.* 1910.

An Aveling and Porter traction engine in Thornton Heath, 1926. The trees in the background are in Grange Park and the fence behind follows the line of Ross Road. The driver was Frank Seaton, a local man, who is leaning on the rear wheel.

An aerial view of the Thornton Heath Pond area, 1928. Silverleigh Road is newly built on the far left with Fairlands Avenue already laid out.

Regulars at the Plough and Harrow, Thornton Heath Pond, before a day out, *c.* 1910.

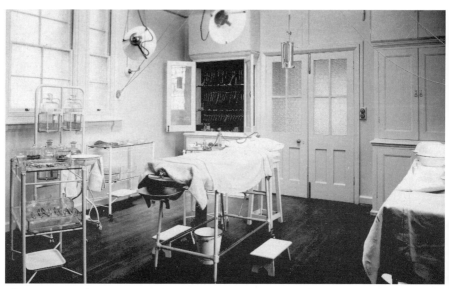

The operating theatre at Mayday Hospital, *c.* 1920. The hospital was originally the workhouse infirmary, the workhouse itself was situated just around the corner in Queens Road (part of the building still survives today).

Thornton Heath Pond, looking from The Wheatsheaf pub across the pond towards Raymead Avenue, *c.* 1928. The pond was filled in in 1953, although a small ornamental pond survived for a while.

St Saviour's Church, St Saviour's Road, shortly after completion in 1867. Tragedy struck just two years later when the first vicar, Revd W. Cameron, died at the age of thirty-seven. The tower and spire of the church were added in 1886.

Brigstock Road, looking up towards Thornton Heath railway station in 1907.

A carnival procession from St Paul's Church turning from Woodville Road into Thornton Heath High Street in June 1926. The carnival was to advertise a fête to be held in connection with the church's restoration fund.

SECTION FOUR

West Croydon, Waddon and Broad Green

A delivery to the Canterbury Arms in Sumner Road (see page 52).

A light monoplane at Waddon in May 1911, probably on the site of what was to become Croydon Airport. The first airfields opened at Waddon in 1915 and 1918.

Looking across the cornfields towards the Waddon Hotel on Stafford Road in 1909. The cornfields were probably part of Coldharbour Farm, which can be seen in the distance on the left. The farm was owned and worked at this time by Robert Bacon.

The workman who found nearly 4,000 Roman coins buried in earthenware pots, standing on the spot in Wandle Road where he discovered them in March 1903. Unfortunately his name is not mentioned in any newspaper reports of the time.

A horse-tram decorated to celebrate the end of the Boer War in 1902. This photograph is thought to have been taken in London Road, possibly at Broad Green.

Digging up potatoes using a patent digger in a field opposite Waddon station in October 1910. Much of the land at Waddon was given over to crop-growing by the two big farms in the area, Waddon Court and Waddon Marsh.

Croydon Airport in the early 1930s, showing both the Waddon Estate and the Waddon Pumping Station in the background. The airport closed in 1959 although the control tower and terminal buildings survive today on Purley Way.

Waddon Pumping Station at Purley Way, 1924. The site is now occupied by The Water Palace and the Hilton Hotel. The line of Haling Park Road and Pampisford Road can just be seen in the distance.

A view of the Turbine House at Croydon B Power Station, Waddon, during its construction in July 1950. The station was recently demolished but its two chimneys were left intact.

The Cafeteria at Purley Way Swimming Pool, 1937. This open-air swimming pool was situated at the junction of Purley Way and Waddon Way, and was a great attraction while it was open between 1935 and 1979.

London Road, Broad Green, c. 1890. This thriving part of London Road is still very much the same today with the Rising Sun on the right and the Half Moon further down on the left.

Taking a break from the harvest at Waddon Court Farm in 1900. The farm was part of the Waddon Court estate which was roughly opposite Waddon station on the other side of what is now the Purley Way. The farm labourers are George Atkinson, Jack Leach, 'Ticky', J. Doulton and J. Coombes.

Ploughing at Canterbury Road in 1884, on land that was part of Waddon Marsh Farm. The farm itself was near the site of Mitcham Road Library and at this time was worked by Mr Cobbett Mighell.

The Canterbury Arms on the corner of Sumner and Lambeth Roads, *c.* 1913. The pub recently changed its name to Nowhere Inn Particular.

Royal Parade, London Road, Broad Green, 1904. The ABC Cinema is now on the left and The Star Hotel (still in existence today as a pub) can be seen in the distance.

Workers at the world-famous Gillett and Johnston Bell Foundry in Union Road, 1912. The foundry supplied the bells for many famous buildings not only in this country but also overseas, for example, in America, Canada and Egypt.

The Accounting and Tabulating ('Acc & Tab') Works at Aurelia Road, 1931.

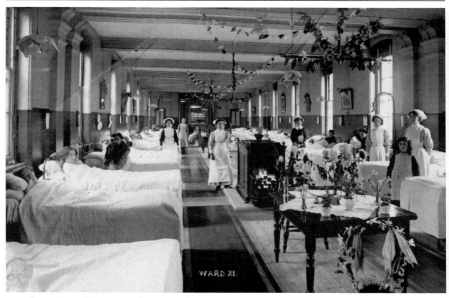

Ward 11, Croydon General Hospital, *c.* 1920.

The Fox and Hounds at West Croydon, decorated for the visit of the Prince and Princess of Wales in May 1896. The occasion was the opening of the new Town Hall in Katharine Street.

Central and South Croydon

Residents of Henry Smith's Almshouses in 1911 (see page 72).

Mr W.C. Berwick-Sayers, Croydon's chief librarian, in July 1930. Mr Berwick-Sayers was in charge of Croydon's libraries between 1915 and 1947 and was well known for his books on local subjects, including *Croydon and the Second World War*.

The staff and pupils of Woodford School, Dingwall Road, *c.* 1900. The school was established in 1867 and numbered among its pupils Dame Peggy Ashcroft, who attended between 1915 and 1924.

Christmas food and entertainment at the Greyhound Hotel in December 1918. This party was one of many given for local children whose fathers had been killed during the First World War.

Old Palace School Hockey Team 1924/5, coached by Miss Goldsmith who is at the centre of the back row. The school occupies the Old Palace, former residence of the Archbishops of Canterbury.

Croydon Hippodrome, Crown Hill, Central Croydon. The Hippodrome opened as a variety theatre in 1910. It became a cinema in 1918 and was converted into a leisure complex in 1972.

A National Baby Week Parade through Croydon, July 1917.

Unemployed men looking for work in the library of Croydon Occupational Centre for Unemployed Men in Church Road in 1933.

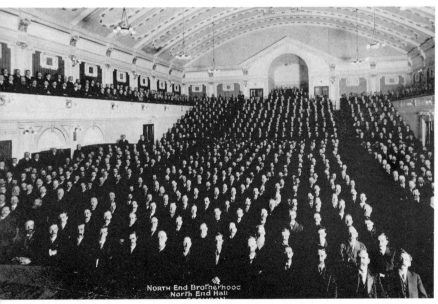

A meeting of the North End Brotherhood in North End Hall, Croydon, in the early 920s. The Brotherhood was founded in January 1912 as a religious movement, with rong social and political interests.

Joshua Allder, 1883. Originally from Walworth, J. Allder set up in business as a linen draper and silk mercer in North End in 1862 when he was only 24. He built his shop up to become one of the major retailers in Croydon until his retirement in 1902, after which the business was sold, although the name has been retained to this day.

The Whitgift School Founder's Day Parade moves past Allders in North End, *c.* 1913.

The Reeves family, *c.* 1900. The family have been in business in Croydon since 1867 and still have a premises at Reeves Corner. Edwin Reeves, the founder of the business, is seated second from the left in the front row. The others in the picture are, back row, left to right: Walter, Edwin and William. Front row, John, Harry and Frederick.

A motor-cycle club meeting outside the Swan and Sugar Loaf in South End, *c.* 1913.

Surrey Street, looking towards Crown Hill, *c.* 1890. The street is one of the oldest shopping areas in Croydon and is the site of the famous daily market. There has been a market in Croydon since 1276.

Poplar Walk, Croydon, looking up towards Wellesley Road in 1920.

The Peace Day Parade goes past the Town Hall in Katharine Street on 28 June 1919. The event was staged to mark the signing of the peace treaty in Versailles which marked the official end of the First World War.

The Old King's Head at the junction of Surrey Street and King Street in 1893, shortly before it was pulled down as part of the High Street Improvement Scheme. William Jackman, the landlord, came to Croydon from Newport on the Isle of Wight.

Camels in North End in 1956, possibly advertising or going to a circus at Fair Field which was an open space at this time.

Duppas Hill, *c*. 1900. Note the sheep grazing in the background.

St John's Road, looking towards the parish church, *c.* 1890. The road is now separated from the church by Roman Way.

A demonstration for the public by Croydon Fire Brigade in April 1910. A newspaper article covering the event states that as the display was nearing its end it had to be stopped as the firemen were called to a real fire.

Tilling motor buses at South Croydon Garage, *c.* 1912.

Croydon Chamber of Commerce excursion on the Thames, *c.* 1900.

The short-lived Croydon Central station in Katharine Street. Between 1868 and 1890 it occupied the site on which the Town Hall now stands and was intended to eradicate the 'long walk' from East Croydon station to central Croydon.

The Croydon Paragon Cycling Club outside the Swan and Sugar Loaf, South End, 1906.

North End, looking south from West Croydon, *c.* 1890. The site of the West Croydon Funeral Establishment on the left is now occupied by Marks and Spencer. The Croydon Free Library, which was the first public library in Croydon, can be seen just past the funeral establishment.

Children playing in Market Street at the back of the old Butter Market in 1892. Market Street ran between Surrey Street and the High Street, and the Butter Market building was later used as the printing office for the newspaper, the *Croydon Chronicle*.

Selsdon Road, South Croydon, *c.* 1920, looking from alongside the Swan and Sugar Loaf towards the junction with Croham Road. A sign on the left warns drivers to 'Drive Cautiously – School' as the original site of Archbishop Tenison's School was further up the road just to the left by the lamp-post.

The car hire department of Moore's Presto Motor Works, Tamworth Road, 1920. Moore's was one of the earliest garages in the area.

Croydon Fire Brigade attending a fire at Pump Pail, *c.* 1910.

Wellesley Road, looking from the junction with George Street towards West Croydon, *c.* 1910. Madame Verrall's costume and mantle shop is the first premises on Wellesley Road on the left and the two gentlemen on the right are standing outside the Public Halls, at the time home of the Croydon Literary and Scientific Institution.

Duppas Hill Road in 1905, looking up towards where the flyover now begins.

Surrey Volunteers (part-time soldiers) relaxing before the visit of the Prince of Wales to open the new town hall in May 1896. Note the Whitgift Almshouses, decorated for the occasion, behind them.

Residents of the Henry Smith's Almhouses in Scarbrook Road celebrating Coronation Day in 1911. Henry Smith was a wealthy London businessman who set up a charitable trust to help the poor of Surrey. The almshouses were opened in 1896.

The Waldrons, *c.* 1913. This road was originally a private estate, which was laid out in the 1850s with houses intended for the wealthy. This photograph shows the gated entrance near Duppas Hill Lane.

The Davis Theatre, High Street, 1937. The cinema was demolished in August 1959 but its name lives on as Davis House, the office block that was built on the site.

Church Street, looking up towards Crown Hill in 1919. The shops on the left side of the street were demolished and rebuilt in about 1930.

South End, looking north towards Croydon in March 1927. The Blue Anchor public house is on the left.

An exhibition billiards match at the Swan and Sugar Loaf Hotel, South Croydon, between the manager, F.J. Upton, and A.F. Peall of the White Horse, Brixton, in October 1910. Peall, who is at the table, was a well-known billiards player and eventually won by 88 points.

SECTION SIX

East Croydon and Addiscombe

Workers at Fremlins Brothers in Dingwall Road (see page 88).

Black Horse Lane, Addiscombe, *c.* 1920.

East Croydon station, 1905. The station was demolished and rebuilt in 1990.

Armed guard at East Croydon station during the First World War. Private William Addiman is on the left and Corporal Coleman, in the middle of his rounds of the guardposts, is on the right (note the motor-cycling gear). During the First World War many important sites such as railway stations and factories had an armed guard in case of invasion.

Cherry Orchard Road, looking towards the junction with Lower Addiscombe Road, *c.* 1920.

The junction of Morland Road, Cherry Orchard Road and Lower Addiscombe Road, *c.* 1910. The Leslie Arms is in the centre of the photograph.

Ashburton Library shortly after its opening in 1927. The library building was originally a convent built by Father Tooth. He was famously imprisoned in 1877 for refusing to let another clergyman take over his services after being told they were too Catholic for Church of England tastes.

Addiscombe railway station, 1899. The station opened in April 1864.

Ashburton Cottages, Lower Addiscombe Road, 1892. The cottages were situated roughly where Baring Road and Lower Addiscombe Road meet.

Part of the Lifeboat Day Parade in July 1908, showing the procession, which has just passed East Croydon station, turning into Cherry Orchard Road from Addiscombe Road.

A group of officers at Addiscombe College, *c.* 1860. The college was the Military Seminary for the East India Company between 1809 and 1861. The officer reading a newspaper on the left appears not to have noticed that the photograph is being taken.

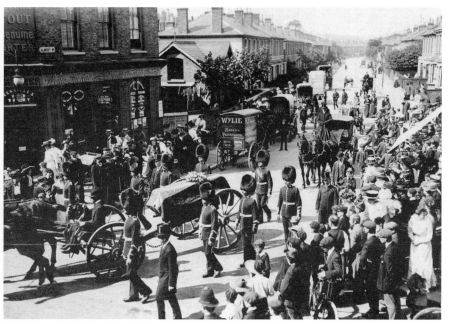

The funeral procession (with full military honours) of a local Crimean War veteran, Mr James Parker, leaving Albert Road and going into Lower Addiscombe Road in August 1910. Mr Parker joined the Grenadier Guards at Croydon in 1853.

An aerial view of Park Hill water tower and recreation ground in 1928, with Stanhope Road winding away on the right. The water tower was built in 1867 and is still one of Croydon's most noticeable landmarks today.

A push-ball match at Addiscombe Tradesmen's Sports Day, July 1911. The locality of this photograph is unknown but it might have been in the grounds of Woodside Convent, where Ashburton Park is today. Presumably the idea of the game was for one team to try and push the ball into the other team's 'goal'.

Elmers Road, Addiscombe, *c.* 1905.

A policeman surveys the damage caused by a bomb dropped from a Zeppelin on Leslie Park Road on 13 October 1915. This air raid killed nine people.

Glendalough in Morland Road, Addiscombe, decorated for the Coronation Carnival in 1902. The house was owned by a prominent local doctor, John Morrison Hobson, who was once a Croydon councillor and who was well known for his articles on archaeology and natural history, which appeared in the *Croydon Advertiser*.

Boys playing cricket at Park Hill Recreation Ground, *c.* 1895. The recreation ground was opened in 1888, although a newspaper report of the time was not impressed with the facilities, calling the recreation ground 'more suitable for a cemetery than a pleasure ground'.

Dalmally Road, Addiscombe, showing extensive bomb damage caused by a V1 flying bomb in July 1944.

Fairfield Road, East Croydon, looking down towards what was Fairfield Path and central Croydon, *c.* 1910. At this time the road was exclusively residential, occupied mostly by professional people.

Addiscombe Road, with Blake Road on the right and Park Hill Road to the left, *c.* 1920.

Canning Road, Addiscombe, *c.* 1920. A lot of the roads in this area were named after men associated with India because of the connection with the East India Company, which had its military college nearby. As well as Canning Road, Clyde, Outram, Elgin and Havelock Roads are all named after famous people connected with the Indian Mutiny.

Fremlins Brothers Family Ale & Stout Stores at No. 54a Dingwall Road, 1921. The gentleman on the right in the doorway is probably William Guthrie, the manager.

Shirley

Members of Shirley Band outside the Sandrock Hotel (see page 91).

A posed photograph for a postcard of Shirley Woods (Addington Hills) in the 1920s. The hills were bought in stages between 1874 and 1919 to be used as a public open space.

An aerial view of Coombe Lodge, Coombe Road, 1924. At this date the house was privately owned by Sir Herbert Brown. Today, the building still stands but is used as a restaurant and hotel.

The Shirley Band outside the Sandrock Hotel in Upper Shirley Road, where they used to practise, in 1895. Mr George Pound, the leader of the band, stands under the drum to the left of the child.

Windmill House, Upper Shirley Road, looking down from Shirley Mill, c. 1925. The house was demolished in 1951 and John Ruskin School occupied the site until 1991 when it too was demolished and replaced by a residential development.

Peace celebrations in Spring Park Road, Shirley, June 1919.

Monks Orchard House at Shirley, 1919. The mansion was built for Lewis Loyd in 185 and demolished in the late 1920s to make way for the Bethlem Royal Hospital.

Shirley Cottage, Wickham Road, 1887. The house was built in the eighteenth century by John Claxton and is still standing today. It was once occupied by Admiral Lord Radstock, one of Nelson's admirals.

An aerial view of Shirley Residential Schools, 1924. The schools were established in 1903 for the board, education and training of Bermondsey poor children. They consisted of thirty-nine detached buildings all named after flowers or plants.

The Shirley Poppy, Wickham Road, in the mid-1930s. The pub was named after the
Shirley Poppy, a special type of poppy developed by Revd William Wilks, who was vicar
of Shirley between 1879 and 1912.

The staff at Heathfield House during the time it was owned by Mr H. Goscher
(1866–1919). The photograph was probably taken in the 1890s.

Mr Moyse's ironmonger's shop on the corner of Barmouth Road and Wickham Road in Shirley, 1932. The Shirley Inn can just be seen in the background.

Bomb damage in Spring Park Road, Shirley, July 1944. The spire of the church of St John the Evangelist is visible in the background.

Mr Raymond Riesco on holiday in Austria in 1937 with his daughters, Jean and Sheila and son, Michael. Mr Riesco owned Heathfield (shown below) between 1925 and 1965. The house and gardens still exist today as part of a public park.

Heathfield, *c.* 1900, with the west wing still standing, to the left of the entrance. This was demolished by Mr Riesco soon after he moved into the house in 1925.

SECTION EIGHT

Addington

Patients at the military hospital at Addington Palace (see page 100).

Addington Vicarage, June 1933. The vicarage was built in 1867 and at this time was occupied by Revd Frederick Nixon. It is now a private house, a new vicarage having been built closer to the church in 1956.

Home Farm, Addington village, covered in wisteria in 1920. The farm was owned by Mr Still, a prominent local landowner, and the man with the dog was his bailiff, Mr Pilcher

The annual race around the Addington Park Estate, April 1910. The race was held for employees at Addington Palace and the winner was Williams the footman (fourth from the left), who covered the 4 mile course in 23½ minutes and won a silver-plated biscuit barrel.

The West Lodge of the Addington Park Estate, c. 1908. The gentleman standing in the garden is Richard Taylor, who worked at Addington Palace, with his wife and child. He is also in the picture above (seventh from the left).

Addington Palace in use as a war hospital during the First World War. Soldiers were often brought straight from the Western Front to be treated at Croydon General Hospital and afterwards recuperated in the war hospitals nearby.

Staff at dinner at Addington Palace War Hospital, c. 1915. As can be seen from this photograph and the one above, the palace must have been one of the grander war hospitals in the borough. It originally took soldiers from France but later specialized in tropical diseases and treated many soldiers from India.

Addington National School, Addington village, 1880. The gentleman with the top hat in the centre is probably the headmaster at that time, Mr R. Fairweather.

Mr W.H. Mills with his family outside their home, Broadcombe Cottage, at Addington, 1923. Mr Mills was a very keen local historian and writer, concentrating especially on Addington.

Arthur Knowlson with his horse and carriages in Addington village yard, 1914. The village yard was next to the Cricketers pub, which is still on its original site today although somewhat expanded.

Maypole Dance at Church Meadow, Addington, August 1923. Olga Kennedy, who is still a resident of Addington, is the tall girl on the left with a pigtail.

Addington Village Cricket Team 1885/6. Back row, left to right: T. Duncan (scorer), V. Thomassett, Revd T. Mylne, M. Coppin, E. Whittle, Russell (umpire). Second row: Walter Sampson, ? Venables, A. Coppin, ? Ironmonger. Front row: R. Coppin, W. Still, F. Coppin.

Addington Pumping Station in Featherbed Lane which was built in 1888. In 1937 it was held responsible for an outbreak of typhoid in Croydon that killed forty-three people. The station was demolished in 1983.

Looking from the top of Gravel Hill, Addington, *c.* 1935. The name Gravel Hill probably refers to the gravel at Addington Hills.

Addington Lodge Farm, Addington, in the 1930s. Much of the land in the background is now covered by New Addington housing estate.

Addington House, 1910. The house still stands today and has been occupied by the same family, the Stills, for over 150 years.

King Henry's Drive during the construction of the New Addington housing estate, July 1953.

Ballard's Farm, Addington. The photograph must have been taken before September 1914 when most of the farm buildings visible were destroyed by fire.

A cottage at Ballards Walk, *c.* 1892. Ballards Walk was probably one of the woodland tracks around Ballards House and Ballards Farm, near where the Royal Russell School now stands.

SECTION NINE

Selsdon and Sanderstead

An early boy scout at Croham Hurst (see page 114).

A lone cyclist beaten by Sanderstead Hill in 1912.

Sanderstead Road, Sanderstead, *c.* 1910. The name Sanderstead means 'sandy place'.

A policeman on the beat at Church Way, Sanderstead, *c*. 1910.

Sanderstead Hill, looking towards Croydon, *c*. 1920. Purley Downs Road is on the left in the foreground.

Old Fox Farm, Sanderstead, 1921. The farmhouse still remains and can be seen in Upper Selsdon Road.

Paddy's Bottom, Sanderstead, 1887. This is now the site of Riddlesdown station.

Purley Oaks Farm, Sanderstead, 1929. The farm was located just off the Brighton Road near the Royal Oak approximately where Norman Avenue is today.

Sanderstead Rectory, 1904. The rectory was once the home of Revd John Randolph, vicar of Sanderstead, who tragically committed suicide in July 1881 possibly because of criticism of the size of his salary in the local newspaper.

The Parade, Sanderstead Road, from a postcard postmarked 1915.

A very quiet-looking Limpsfield Road, Sanderstead, c. 1925.

James Braid, the well-known golf professional, plays the first shot at the opening of Croham Hurst Golf Course in April 1912.

Selsdon Park Hotel, *c.* 1930. The house was started by William Coles, who was eventually declared bankrupt so it was completed by the MP George Smith, who bought it in 1809. It has been an hotel since 1924.

Old Farleigh Road, Selsdon, *c*. 1925.

Croham Hurst, 1910. The Hurst was bought as an open space for local people from the Whitgift Foundation by Croydon Corporation in 1901.

Coulsdon, Purley and Kenley

Road labourers in Purley in 1895 (see page 119).

Bell tents housing soldiers overflowing on to Coulsdon Common from the Guards Depot in Caterham during the First World War. The photograph was taken from the old mill on the common probably during the early part of the war when recruitment was at its height.

Women gathering for the Coronation Dinner of King Edward VII at Coulsdon Court Farm in 1902.

May Day celebrations outside the Red Lion in Coulsdon, 1905. The pub was an important coaching inn during the nineteenth century with forty stage-coaches a day stopping there at peak times.

An imposing-looking Cane Hill Hospital in Coulsdon, 1936. The hospital was opened as a mental institution in 1883 and closed in March 1992. At the time of writing the future of the site is still undecided.

Purley Council Vehicle Depot in Brighton Road, 1926. The vehicles belong to the Highways and Public Health Department.

The Warehousemans' and Drapers' School at Russell Hill, Purley, *c.* 1914. The school later moved to Ballards, and is now the Royal Russell School.

Workmen at Foxley Lane taking a break to pose for the camera, 1895.

The ancient ceremony of Beating the Bounds, which traditionally marked the boundaries of the parish, being performed in 1908. The group is at the junction of Woodmansterne Road and Russell Hill Road in Purley.

A very early motor caravan in Coulsdon, July 1910. Other pictures in this series show staff from Cane Hill Asylum in tents and caravans, so this may have been some sort o event connected with the asylum.

Great Roke Farm, Kenley, 1889. The farm was formerly known as Standing Lodge (see also p. 122).

Mr Marwick the butcher and his delivery cart in Purley, *c.* 1900. The Marwicks had a butcher's business in the area from the late 1880s, when their shop opened at No. 10 Whytecliffe Road, Purley, until 1972.

Russell Hill Road, Purley, *c.* 1905.

Great Roke Farm, Kenley, 1897. The flooding was caused by an overflow of the Bourne River called the Bourne Flow. The farm was owned at this time by Thomas Stuchberry.

A very rough-looking Foxley Lane, looking down towards Purley, c. 1905. The narrow Foxley Lane probably derives from Purley's original name, Foxley Hatch.

righton Road, Purley, with Russell Hill Road off to the right, 1905.

hildren playing at Riddlesdown Common, *c.* 1910. The common was bought by the orporation of London in 1883 as an open space for the enjoyment of Londoners.

People gathering at the Rose and Crown, Kenley, possibly for a day out, *c.* 1903. Th sign reading 'Nalder & Collyers' refers to an old Croydon brewery established in 1849.

'The Wheelwright's Mortuary' on Coulsdon Common, June 1930. This was probabl the nickname given to Thomas Rivers' workshop, which was situated on Coulsdo Common from the 1880s.

Hurdle making in Inwood, Coulsdon, 1887. Hurdle making was a prominent local industry at this time, especially in the Old Coulsdon area. The name Inwood survives today as Inwood Avenue.

Milking time at Welcomes Farm, Kenley, *c.* 1910. The farm stood roughly where Kearton Close is today.

'The Old Man's' Temperance Refreshment Rooms and Hotel on the corner of Lion Green Road and Brighton Road in Coulsdon, *c.* 1916. The owner was D. Coppard and he is thought to be the old man who gave the place its nickname.

Acknowledgements

I would like to acknowledge the help of the following in the compilation of this book:

The staff of Croydon Local Studies Library, Steve Roud and Margaret Mumford and the borough's archivist, Oliver Harris; Ken Maggs for his help with captions; John Gent for his guidance and advice; and Olga Kennedy both for the loan of photographs and help with captions. Olga Kennedy's photographs, which are not in the collection at the Local Studies Library, are on pp. 98, 102 and 105a.

Copies of most of the photographs in this book are in the photographic collection at Croydon Local Studies Library, but the author would like to express his thanks to the following for permission to use their photographs:

Sue Banfield • John Crook • *Croydon Advertiser*
Croydon Archives Service • Croydon Natural History and Scientific Society
Mrs V. Feist • Imperial War Museum • London Transport Executive
Mr A. Moyles • Purley Public Library (photographs held at Purley and not at
the Local Studies Library are on pp. 108, 109, 110, 111a, 116b, 117, 118,
119a, 120, 122b, 124, 125a, 126) • M.W. Reeves • Joe Seaton
J.W. Sparrowe • Jean Thorpe